Billionaires mindset

LEARN THE WINNING MINDSET OF THE SUPER RICH

Copyright © 2018. All Rights Reserved.

No part of this publication may be reproduced, distributed, or transmitted in any form or by any means, including photocopying, recording, or other electronic or mechanical methods, or by any information storage and retrieval system without the prior written permission of the publisher, except in the case of very brief quotations embodied in critical reviews and certain other noncommercial uses permitted by copyright law.

Why You Should Read This Book

Mindset is what differs the successful from the unsuccessful. Because of that, this book delves into the minds of billionaires who went from zero to super success. They did so by creating multi-billion wealth for other people. The goal is to show how YOU can adopt their mindset on your path towards a worthy goal in life.

...

Table of Contents

Why You Should Read This Book

Table of Contents

Chapter 1. Introduction

Chapter 2. Naveen Jain (multibillion innovator

Chapter 3. Grant Cardone (real estate)

Chapter 4. Daniel Ek (Spotify)

Chapter 5. Elon Musk (Tesla, solar energy, populate Mars)

Chapter 6. Richard Branson (Virgin, Aeroplanes, space travel, music)

Chapter 7. conclusion

Chapter 8. Disclaimer

Naveen Jain (multibillion innovator)

If anybody feels absolutely right at the core of my being when listening to his words, feeling his energy and tuning in to his spirit, it is the multibillion entrepreneur Naveen Jain. Because of that, I feel warmly honored to present one of the greatest entrepreneurs and entrepreneur mindsets the world today has to offer.

Personal history

Naveen Jain was born in 1959 in poor areas in India. In 1979 he arrived to USA from India with 5 dollars in his pocket. Then earning an engineering degree at the Indian Institute of Technology in Roorkee. Growing up as a poor kid in India he had little knowledge of entrepreneurship, but he looked up to business people who made it, especially Bill Gates. Jain married in 1988 and moved with his family to Silicon Valley and worked for some startups before joining Microsoft one year later.

Yet, after some time in the USA he was about to give up. It was winter, cold and wet, and he decided to go back to India. As he was about to leave, an old friend called him and heard about his plans to leave the US. The old friend got a little upset and let Naveen know that he is smart and should stay and try to make business in the USA. A whole lot of years later, the same friend called Naveen when he was a successful billionaire. Naveen did not recognise the voice of his old friend and asked how he could help, secretly hoping to get rid of this person. The old friend congratulated Naveen for his success. Now Naveen recognised his old friend and wanted to return the favor of his friend, sincerely asking how he can halp and if there is anything he needs. But alas, the friend needed nothing. Naveen never got the opportunity to return the favor. It bothered him deeply, and still to this day Mr Jain devotes a large portion of his life to paying back his debt to the people who made him successful. As a consequence, he inspires and teaches young entrepreneurs to become more successful. Naveen now has three children, Ankur, Priyanka, and Neil, and they all make a significant impact on the world today. His has founded six companies, and they all bring massive value to a huge number of people.

Business background

What makes Naveen Jain unique is his remarkable success in bransches that are very different. He founded six companies, all of them reaching mega success in terms of profits and value added to the world. In 1996, Naveen Jain had a rather promising career as an employee at Microsoft. Then he terminated his employment, went home to his family members and let them know that there will be no paycheck. The same year he co-founded InfoSpace together with a handful of employees at Microsoft. The business idea was to develop directories for telephones and e-mails. He got that idea from studying the businesses that were out there. Suddenly he saw a company that was targeting websites and users of mobile devices. He thought that is should be a great idea to combine the use of computers with mobile devices. He called the CEO of that company and with full confidence declared that he would make the CEO go out of business. He will take over! The CEO asked how he would to that. Without hesitation, Mr Jain replied that he will be up before him in the mornings and take his first customers of that day, and he will work later in the evenings and take over the last customers that call in. Said and done, Jain's net worth grew to $8 billion as InfoSpace provided stock market information, phone directories, games, and maps to websites and manufacturers of mobile devices. InfoSpace did not fall into the trap of getting external funding and instead used partnerships to increase profits. The company went public in 1998 and raised $75 million in the offering.

Intelius was co founded in 2003. In one year, the company quickly grew its revenues to $18 by providing information about specific individuals. Revenues increased rapidly and the company was sold in 2015 with great profits. In 2006, Jain founded Talentwise, who offers hiring process management solutions in North America. The company was sold in 2016.

In 2010 Jain co-founded Moon Express to mine valuable materials like cobalt, platinum, gold, and Helium-3, which is a fuel for nuclear energy. Since the south pole of the moon contains massive resources of water, it is planned to be used for rocket fuel on missions to Mars and other planets. The plan is to have established human colonies on the moon by 2022.

As a founder and CEO of Bluedot and Viome in 2015 and 2016, Mr Jain is analyzing clients' gut flora to give dietary advice and cure diseases. Naveen's point is that a large number of diseases can be derived to a faltering gut flora. A better gut flora composition can therefore cure diseases. This icludes disorders that traditionally are not associated with the human gut flora composition.

Additionally, he is active in Kairos Society, Xprize Foundation and Singularity University, which are networks and enterprices that help entrepreneurs and scientists to collaborate and bring revolutionary products to the market.

Mindset

Naveen is a strong advocate of unconditional giving. He explains that a leader needs to love not only his customers but also his employees like as if they are his children. These children gets his unconditional love no matter what. Naveen's strong focus on giving value with little empasis on taking gives us the opportunity to give back. This does not mean that Naveen is uninterested in profit. He often makes it clear that "doing good and doing well is not mutually exclusive". In other words, he expects massive profit from his enterprices that do good for the world.

This integration of the financial and the spiritual realms that seem so separate is what makes me feel that he is a true leader. This expression of his higher self in the entrepreneur world seems to trigger an unquenchable enthusiasm, making him work from early morning to late evening and rarely take a day off. In addition to enthusiasm, Naveen shows an immense curiosity and thirst for new knowledge, which makes him intellectually rich. He goes up at 4.30 in the morning and devotes his first three waking hours to catching up with emails and reading, reading, and more reading. So what does he read? Scientific journals, books, blogs, and cutting edge information about his various areas of interest. This brings us to his business strategies.

Naveen Jain's business strategies

Having been remarkably successful in several enterprises, without anyone failing. One may wonder how he did it, step by step. As he says in this [YouTube link] video clip, he puts a lot of faith on innovations for bringing humanity forward. Also, he enters new markets as an outsider. Contrary to an expert, Naveen claims that an outsider can look at things with different eyes and find tremendous value through entirely new solutions.

More specifically, Naveen's success strategy is to read for hours every day and become very informed on cutting edge research in different fields. Then connect the dots between these fields. New solutions and innovations are the new dots. In this process, Naveen finds a big vision that brings humanity forward. One example of this vision is to eliminate a large portion of the diseases that exist today, by impacting the gut ...something. By presenting such revolutionary goals he easily attracts people that want to work for him. It is far more compelling and inspiring to work for a great goal than continuing as an employee in a company that is getting old. That is why Mr Jain is so good at attracting people who want to be hired. More concretely, Jain may search for new information on the internet and in social media. He uses these media to ask for help on information from experts in that field. He mentions that most people want to help others, and because of that he asks for help, and as a result he gets a lot of response from experts that can bring his projects forward. Also, in this way he gets lots of connections with highly informed individuals. At other times he simply picks up the phone and calls experts, telling them about his vision. Since the vision is so compelling, he attracts these experts to his team. He is also a passionate public speaker and attracts attention and new connections that way. In this YouTube video, Naveen goes into a more detailed description on how he attracts new partnerships.

Grant Cardone (real estate)

Grant Cardone is a motivational speaker, sales trainer, business owner, author and radio host of The Cardone Zone. Grant is a multi-millionaire who runs one of the worlds best sales training companies, he owns several businesses and has a real estate portfolio of around $350 million.

Grant Cardone is an individual who demands you to go all in and do all that you can at unexpected levels so that you can live life on your own terms. His quotes are powerful and demand that you push yourself to be the best you that you can be. If you develop Grant's work ethic within yourself then success is inevitable.

Personal history

Grant Cardone is an American author, sales trainer, real estate Investor, and motivational speaker. He is New York Times best-selling author, and radio show host of The Cardone Zone. Grant is also known for television series Turnaround King (2011).

Grant Cardone was born on March 21, 1958, in Lake Charles, Louisiana, USA. His nationality is American and ethnicity is North American.

His father's name is Curtis Louis Cardone and mother Concetta Neil Cardone. Grant is born the twin. He is the fourth of five children. His twin brother name is Gary Cardone.

Grant did his schooling from LaGrange High School in Lake Charles and went to McNeese State University for his graduation with a Bachelor of Science Degree in Accounting.

While in the university, he was awarded as the McNeese State University Distinguished Alumnus Award in 2010.

After completing his graduation, Grant Cardone moved to Chicago to work for a sales-training company. For his career growth, Grant lived in many cities in the United States and later moved to Houston, Texas. He again shifted to La Jolla, California for 12 years.

Later, Grant moved his offices from California to Miami Beach. Grant choose not to pursue the field of accounting and moved into automobile sales. Grant also became CEO of Freedom Motorsports Group Inc.

Grant is also an author. He wrote seven books Sell To Survive, The Closer's Survival Guide, If You're Not First, You're Last, The 10X Rule, Sell or Be Sold, The Millionaire Booklet and Be Obsessed or Be Average. Grant worked with Atlas Media Corp and developed a reality television series for the National Geographic Channel named Turnaround King.

Grant holds a real estate portfolio valued at around $350 million. He owns many businesses like Cardone Enterprises, The Cardone Group, and Cardone Acquisitions.

Grant was named 1 of the 25 Marketing Influencers to Watch in 2017 by Forbes. Grant is a member of the Church of Scientology. His company Freedom Motorsports sponsored NASCAR drivers and helped to promote Dianetics and Scientology.

Business background

Since the age of 15, Cardone had been studying the ins and outs of real estate. During his childhood, he and his father regularly visited different pieces of property as a family outing activity, and over time his interest in buying buildings developed. To this day, shopping real estate is still something he enjoys doing with his wife and children.

In 1981, at the age of 22, Cardone graduated from college with an accounting degree. Despite wanting to immediately acquire properties, he delayed doing so for a few years. This allowed him to grow the money that he would later use to make investments. Additionally, the delay gave Cardone the time to soak up as much as he could on the subject of real estate.

In an October 2014 episode of his real estate show, Cardone shared that a lot of his education – "understanding different terms such as net operating income (NOI), what a pro forma is, and what a good market looks like" – came not from academic study but from actually "looking at different deals, and meeting agents." In fact, Cardone has never read anything on real estate investing: he replaced the knowledge that can be found in books with knowledge that can be attained by actually looking at listings in different markets. (For more, see How Much Money Do You Need to Invest in Real Estate?)

His First Deal

At 29, Cardone finally put his more than 14 years of real estate studying into practice. He bought a single-family property in Houston that initially did well. However, after a few months, the tenants left, and Cardone's cash flow dried up. He often jokes about the experience saying, "My occupancy rate moved from 100% right down to 0%." He hated the fact that he had to lessen the focus on his main business in order to find new tenants. Afraid that this situation would recur, Cardone quickly sold the property, broke even and swore that he would never purchase single-family residential real estate as an investment ever again.

Subsequent Acquisitions

Cardone's second acquisition did not take place until five years later. During that time, he continued to accumulate cash as well as increase his property investing knowledge base. His first multifamily-property deal was a 38-unit complex in San Diego. Cardone acquired the property for $1.9 million, making a down payment of $350,000. Just over a month later, he acquired another complex.

Cardone continued to purchase more complexes – at first, one at a time, though the pace later picked up. In 2012, Cardone Acquisitions made what was dubbed Florida's largest private party acquisition of multifamily real estate, a portfolio of 1,016 apartment, spread over five apartment communities, for a total of $59 million.

His real estate holdings are based in Alabama, Arizona, California, Florida, Georgia, North Carolina, Tennessee and Texas.

Mindset

Cardone had a business mindset, now you can use them to build your empire. Here's what he had to say.

1. Compartmentalizing doesn't work.

When you are building your empire (or even just one business), it takes major focus and obsession. Instead of being obsessed with negative things, get obsessed about your business. Cardone literally saved his own life by switching from drug obsession to business obsession.

Compartmentalizing your business into strict operating hours doesn't work if you want to be successful. Successful people don't just turn off their brain and completely forget about their business for two days over the weekend, or even when they are out for a night at the movies.

"When you drop in on something, to make it successful, there is no balance in that moment. To be obsessed is a good thing, not a bad thing", said Cardone.

2. You can do many things at once.

Burning out does not happen because you are doing too many things. Look at Elon Musk who is building electric cars while finding a way to go to Mars.

"People burn out because their life is not interesting enough," said Cardone.

Cardone explained that most people don't have enough going on to keep them excited. Many people don't have problems or challenges big enough to make them feel alive, vibrant and excited again like a child experiencing something for the first time.

So the next time someone tells you to focus on one thing and one thing only, ask them if they have heard of Elon Musk, Grant Cardone, or Google.

3. Incredible people find their inner superstar.

One of the most important things I learned from Cardone was that super successful people don't follow the crowd. Instead, they constantly challenge conventional thinking and wake themselves up when everyone else is doing the average thing.

Find that inner superhero or sports superstar in you-- the one that knows they can do incredible things. No matter what, utilize the energy behind those things in your business. It doesn't mean you have to be a professional baseball player or NBA all-star, but you can use the energy behind that in your business life.

"I wanted to be a catcher. The catcher is the control freak of the diamond; he runs the game. He runs the pitcher; he's running everything that goes on. So even though I couldn't be a baseball player, I'm able to still grab that part of me that wants to lead and guide", said Cardone.

4. People have to know who you are.

Cardone is popular on Facebook, Twitter, Instagram, Snapchat and YouTube, just to name a few. He's actually on dozens of different platforms in total. By being on all of these platforms constantly, you get in front of people, and they don't forget you.

And don't worry about people not liking you. Inevitably people may not like you, and that's ok. It's impossible to build a big brand--whether it's your company or your personal brand--without getting negative feedback. It happens, and you have to be ok with that.

"I don't have a favorite platform. My favorite would be that wherever you go, you see my face. I don't care that you like me or love me or hate me, what's important to me is that you know me," said Cardone.

5. Have people around you that are doing well.

If you are the smartest person in the room, maybe you are in the wrong room.

Instead of putting a bunch of 'yes' men around you that just want to hang out with someone successful, try surrounding yourself with other rockstars.

Cardone makes a point of surrounding himself with other rock stars so that he is forced to be on the top of his game.

"I want people around me to also be the rockstars," said Cardone.

At the end of the day, obsession is the name of the game for Cardone. Like Cardone, you can have it all.

Business strategies

Grant Cardone is a self made multimillionaire who changed his financial status by changing his mind, attitude and strategies. He is a successful best selling author, correspondent for various TV networks and hods a $350 million real estate portfolio. From his success story he has managed to inspire, mentor and educate a lot of people on how to grow their wealth. What makes him great is the fact that he does not keep the success strategies and techniques to himself but has shared it with the world. There are a lot of things one can learn from Grant Cordone, and these are the most important ones

1. Commitment

In order for you to accomplish anything you set your mind to, the most crucial factor is commitment. How much time, money and resources are you committing to it? For Grant Cardone to make all the money he has, the first thing he had to do was committing to the course. He committed his time and mind to becoming successful at what he did. Stay committed to your course without giving up or giving in. Do all you can to make sure that you see the results you need. Above everything else be committed to increasing your wealth.

2. Mind renewal

This is done by staying positive no matter the problems and challenges you may go through and getting rid of average thinking. Do not think in the line of settling just because you have enough to afford yourself or your family a little extra pleasure. Do not settle until you are sure you are more than capable to provide yourself and your family the greatest that life can offer and that you have exhausted all the opportunities you need to build your wealth. Truth be told, new opportunities are arising day and night. Learn to not settle for average but the best

3. Shifting focus from spending to investing

This is by far the greatest way to build your wealth. Most people think in the line of spending whatever little money they have instead of thinking of investing it so that it can multiply and become plenty. Whenever you have money, search for investing opportunities that are within your financial range and invest. Within no time you will be having more than enough and you will still have enough to invest. The money you get from your first investments, divide the profit into two. One half for your expenditure and the other half expand your investments in terms of shares. Spending does not give you anything in return but investing makes you richer by the day.

4. Creating multiple flows of income

This is also another great way of building your wealth. Depending on one source of income will not cut it in a world where the economy keeps fluctuating. Having multiple sources of income is like having a backup generator when there is a power shortage. When one source of income is unstable, the other source will save you. If all the sources of income are more than stable your net income will be so much greater than when having one stable source of income.

5. Do not show off

When your financial status starts to improving, do not focus on showing off by buying the most expensive stuff in the market like cars and houses. Focus on always being in time for your meetings, appointments and work. Build your wealth and let it be stable enough to afford you the best that life has to offer.

6. Create attention

In his selling summit in 2015, Grant Cardone emphasized on creating attention for your products and services. The more the attention you create the more consumers for your products and services will be. This sill not hurt your pocket. As a matter of fact it is really good for your pocket. Sell your products and services by packaging it in a way that is attractive and enticing to the public.

Daniel Ek (Spotify)

Daniel founded his first company in 1997 at the age of 14, when he joined a group of people to attend counseling orders via the Internet, as well as a web hosting company pages outside his room. Two years later, he came across Google and tried to go to work in the company by sending his CV, but he was not accepted because he did not have a degree.

The Google incident would brand him forever to such an extent that influenced his recruitment policy, moving away from the idea of Google to hire only graduates from prestigious universities, Daniel opted for the diversity of cultures, gender, ethnicity, thinking, income and education. In fact, following the rejection of Google, he tried to create a search engine to compete, but could not make it.

Ek created Advertigo, an advertising, web ads, postcards and mobile design application, which was acquired by TradeDoubler, a company owned by Martin Lorentzon, who years later would become his partner in the Spotify creation

Personal history

Daniel Ek, (born February 21, 1983, Stockholm, Sweden), Swedish entrepreneur who in 2006 cofounded Spotify, an

Internet music-streaming service that provides listeners with legal, ad-supported access to millions of songs, rejecting traditional models of downloading and eliminating per-song costs.

Business background

Ek grew up in Ragsved, near Stockholm, and, as a teenager, he created Web sites for businesses and ran Web hosting services out of his bedroom. He dropped out of college and worked for several Web-based companies before founding Advertigo, an online marketing firm that he sold in 2006 to the Swedish company Tradedoubler. He then established Spotify with Tradedoubler's cofounder, Martin Lorentzon, and became CEO. Ek's innovative business model for providing access to music online differed from other services in that it did not involve charging for song downloads. Spotify customers could listen to online streaming music for free if they were willing to allow display or audio advertising. For $5 or $10 a month in subscription fees, however, consumers could avoid the advertisements.

From the outset, the music industry expressed little enthusiasm for Ek's innovation, because Spotify's license to stream music earned the industry far less revenue per song than it got from a music download service such as Apple Inc.'s iTunes. Ek retorted that Spotify discouraged online music piracy by providing a low-cost alternative and that the service would, over time, generate substantial royalties for the music industry. Despite such reservations, Spotify launched in 2008 and quickly became popular with both users and investors. By 2010 venture capital money was beginning to flow in to Spotify, and some analysts estimated that the service's potential value was as much as $4 billion. In 2012 Spotify had 18 million songs and more than 20 million monthly active users, though not all were paying subscribers. Five years later, however, the site featured more than 35 million songs and had nearly 160 million monthly active users, more than 70 million of whom were subscribers. Amid this incredible growth, Ek oversaw Spotify's initial public offering in April 2018. In an unusual move, the company offered no new stock, and instead only existing shares were made available. After the first day of trading, Spotify had a market value of about $27 billion.

Mindset

Try to cope with your low-variance problems, said daniel

Taking an in-depth look at the choice many great entrepreneur as to make and I split them into low-variance problems and high-variance problems. Among the mistakes business people make is this: as a more substantial company, easy and simple thing to purchase is the low-variance problems. Low-variance problems will be the ones which bring relatively little benefits if you are best in category, but there's a boat load of downside unless you do them sufficiently.

An ideal example is paying wages. If you're the best in the entire world at paying incomes, the huge benefits in being the best versus being just fine aren't that high. People just be prepared to get paid over a certain time. But if you miss that night out, then you are screwed. It really is, really bad and you have a severe morale concern.

I find that a lot of entrepreneurs are very good in the high-variance bucket, but it is the low-variance part that people under-invest in. For example, until just lately - and I didn't pay much focus on this - we were working by using an ERP system that quit being backed by Microsoft in 2001. We remain operating that thing even today.

We are most likely 10 times bigger now than whoever has ever before used that thing, therefore the cost for all of us to switch are incredibly high. 200 people will work on this for some time now. That which was a fairly trivial decision in the past now becomes this multi-year thing where we must migrate everyone to this new system and keep carefully the two systems working in parallel.

A Ceo must change careers every 2 yrs

There will vary skill sets for each and every phase of a company. One for when you yourself have just started the business, one for if you are 50 people, one for if you are 150 people, one for if you are 1,000 people and one for if you are 10,000 people.

I usually notify individuals who I change careers every 2 yrs. I began as the janitor, i quickly became the merchandise guy, i quickly became the HR person, i quickly became this content one who negotiated all the offers. There are various phases by having a company's life where you, as the creator, must wear numerous hats, and that is really hard. You need to be functional as a person to have the ability to do that. I believe this is exactly what people get incorrect.

Business strategies

Face your proper blunders, and move fast to repair things

Daniel Ek: "For a long time, Spotify disregarded the impact of mobile. Desktop was ruler and we hadn't even qualified a mobile product apart from reduced one. That's because we viewed the entire world as a location where everyone would use desktop and smartphone alongside one another. We thought it was a good idea to 'upsell' the mobile product."

"For an extended period, that was great because whenever people wished to use Spotify on the mobile device, that they had to cover the merchandise. But because we followed a freemium model, we're highly reliant on also having free users build relationships the service. As the planet transferred towards mobile, definitely that free area of the funnel vanished."

The majority of our investors observed our income figures and alteration rate feel the rooftop, while we were recognizing that people made a tactical mistake and we'd to reinvent the complete company to repair it. It required us over 18 months, as we'd to return to the music industry and inform them that finished . we used to charge money for would have to be given free of charge as well. That had not been a fairly easy sell. We informed our partners that people would find out a fresh way for folks to cover the product.

It had been like transitioning out the machines mid-flight. But if we wouldn't did it, half a year later we may have passed away as an organization. That basically was a defining point in time and this was as later as 2013. For what it's worthy of: I feel that every great company has at least three near-death experience.

Many people speak about the willingness to own failures, but I hate failures. I don't believe you should affect to make failures. I believe it's fine to make errors, but by enough time they become real failures, you almost certainly should have uncovered them.

The way I believe relating to this is that people constantly must make wagers where we're able to be incorrect about the methods, but maybe we wouldn't be incorrect about the target. If we are quick and agile, we can move fast to repair things. So, we do make mistakes on the way but the entire project didn't conclude becoming a inability.

Make a few tactical bets rather than doing 100 things and expect the best

As you feel bigger, one of the issues you will face is that you'll require to be growing at 100% or even more for multiple years, specially when you have VC's buying you.

What will happen if you get almost any traction is the fact regulations of gravity begins tugging you down. It gets harder and harder to develop fast. So actually, you will make bigger and bigger wagers to have even a remote potential for making that expansion number.

After some time you may start making plenty of small wagers in the trust that a few of them come out big, or you merely make considerably bigger bets in proportions but make fewer of these. There are very a few companies that execute a whole lot of small wagers - plus some of these play out - and then there are a few, like Amazon . com, who say, 'Hey, India is a major guess for us' and then devote several billion dollars and expect the best in several years' time.

I believe we are looking for our way, but we never liked doing 100 things simultaneously and expect the best. I cannot even produce even 100 different goals, so I'd somewhat make a few proper bets and ensure that we don't are unsuccessful on those.

That, I believe, is an essential distinction i don't see startup internet marketers getting. Failing is not at all something you should shoot for. Making blunders is okay, if you make sure they are quick and cheap.

Your first employees are the main hires you'll make

In the first times, you typically retain the services of people that you understand that are good. You do not put vacancies on employment board. In the event that you find the first people you retain meticulously, you'll go away the first 'life or death'-faze of your enterprise. That is the main thing that people look for whenever we acquire companies and move them in: getting the right team.

The next thing gets that team to satisfy the right objective. 'Objective' may possibly be translated into 'being uncooperative on the eye-sight and the challenge you want to solve, but being adaptable on the facts of how you are handling that problem'. Those will be the two most significant things for all of us.

You must display for factors like enthusiasm when recruiting. I am not stating that everyone in Spotify is hardcore into music. That isn't important. Sometimes the objective itself can be interpreted diversely by individuals, maybe it's a subset of the objective that is super-appealing to someone.

If you're a data scientist, you may well not care much about music, nevertheless, you care about how precisely people connect to music, which becomes the matter that latches you on and enables you to believe that this is something you must understand.

Elon Musk (Tesla, solar energy, populate Mars)

As CEO of SpaceX and Tesla, founder of The Boring Company, and cofounder of OpenAI, Musk seems to be everywhere all at once, pushing all kinds of incredible new technologies. He's said he won't be happy until we've escaped Earth and colonized Mars.

Between space rockets, electric cars, solar batteries, research into killer robots, and the billions he's made along the way, Musk is basically a real-life Tony Stark — which is why he served as an inspiration for "Iron Man."

But it wasn't always easy for Musk. Here's how he went from getting bullied in school to small-time entrepreneur to CEO of two major companies that seem like they're straight out of science fiction

Personal history

Elon Musk was born on June 28th, 1971, in Pretoria, South Africa.

His father said he's "always been an introvert thinker."

"Where a lot of people would go to a great party and have a great time and drink and talk about all sorts of things like rugby or sport, you would find Elon had found the person's library and was going through their books," Musk's dad, electronics engineer Errol Musk, said.

Musk's mother is a professional dietitian and model.

Maye Musk, a Canadian national, has appeared on boxes of Special K cereal and the cover of Time magazine.

After their parents divorced in 1979, the nine-year-old Musk and his younger brother, Kimbal, decided to live with their father.

After their parents divorced in 1979, the nine-year-old Musk and his younger brother, Kimbal, decided to live with their father.

Musk and his brother, Kimbal YouTube, Bloomberg News

Musk felt sorry for his father, whose three children had gone to live with their mother after the divorce. It wasn't until after the move was made that his notoriously troubled relationship with his dad began to emerge.

"It was not a good idea," Musk said in a recent Rolling Stone interview about moving in with his father.

In 1983, at the age of 12, Musk sold a simple game called "Blastar" to a computer magazine for $500

Business background

At age 17, in 1989, Elon Musk moved to Canada to attend Queen's University and avoid mandatory service in the South African military. He left in 1992 to study business and physics at the University of Pennsylvania. He graduated with an undergraduate degree in economics and stayed for a second bachelor's degree in physics.

After leaving Penn, Elon Musk headed to Stanford University in California to pursue a PhD in energy physics. However, his move was timed perfectly with the Internet boom, and he dropped out of Stanford after just two days to become a part of it, launching his first company, Zip2 Corporation. An online city guide, Zip2 was soon providing content for the new websites of both The New York Times and the Chicago Tribune. In 1999, a division of Compaq Computer Corporation bought Zip2 for $307 million in cash and $34 million in stock options.

PayPal

In 1999, Musk co-founded X.com, an online financial services/payments company. An X.com acquisition the following year led to the creation of PayPal as it is known today, and in October 2002, PayPal was acquired by eBay for $1.5 billion in stock. Before the sale, Musk owned 11 percent of PayPal stock.

Founder of SpaceX

Musk founded his third company, Space Exploration Technologies Corporation, or SpaceX, in 2002 with the intention of building spacecraft for commercial space travel. By 2008, SpaceX was well established, and NASA awarded the company the contract to handle cargo transport for the International Space Station—with plans for astronaut transport in the future—in a move to replace NASA's own space shuttle missions.

Falcon 9 Rockets

On May 22, 2012, Musk and SpaceX made history when the company launched its Falcon 9 rocket into space with an unmanned capsule. The vehicle was sent to the International Space Station with 1,000 pounds of supplies for the astronauts stationed there, marking the first time a private company had sent a spacecraft to the International Space Station. Of the launch, Musk was quoted as saying, "I feel very lucky. ... For us, it's like winning the Super Bowl."

In December 2013, a Falcon 9 successfully carried a satellite to geosynchronous transfer orbit, a distance at which the satellite would lock into an orbital path that matched the Earth's rotation. In February 2015, SpaceX launched another Falcon 9 fitted with the Deep Space Climate Observatory (DSCOVR) satellite, aiming to observe the extreme emissions from the sun that affect power grids and communications systems on Earth.

In March 2017, SpaceX saw the successful test flight and landing of a Falcon 9 rocket made from reusable parts, a development that opened the door for more affordable space travel. A setback came in November 2017, when an explosion occurred during a test of the company's new Block 5 Merlin engine. SpaceX reported that no one was hurt, and that the issue would not hamper its planned rollout of a future generation of Falcon 9 rockets.

The company enjoyed another milestone moment in February 2018 with the successful test launch of the powerful Falcon Heavy rocket. Armed with additional Falcon 9 boosters, the Falcon Heavy was designed to carry immense payloads into orbit and potentially serve as a vessel for deep space missions. For the test launch, the Falcon Heavy was given a payload of Musk's cherry-red Tesla Roadster, equipped with cameras to "provide some epic views" for the vehicle's planned orbit around the sun.

BFR Mission to Mars

In September 2017, Musk presented an updated design plan for his BFR (an acronym for either "Big F---ing Rocket" or "Big Falcon Rocket"), a 31-engine behemoth topped by a spaceship capable of carrying at least 100 people. He revealed that SpaceX was aiming to launch the first cargo missions to Mars with the vehicle in 2022, as part of his overarching goal of colonizing the Red Planet.

In March 2018, the entrepreneur told an audience at the annual South by Southwest festival in Austin, Texas, that he hoped to have the BFR ready for short flights early the following year, while delivering a knowing nod at his previous problems with meeting deadlines.

The following month, it was announced that SpaceX would construct a facility at the Port of Los Angeles to build and house the BFR. The port property presented an ideal location for SpaceX, as its mammoth rocket will only be movable by barge or ship when completed.

Internet Satellites

In late March 2018, SpaceX received permission from the U.S. government to launch a fleet of satellites into low orbit for the purpose of providing Internet service. Ideally, the system would make broadband service more accessible for people in rural areas, while also boosting competition in heavily populated markets that are typically dominated by one or two providers. Critics countered that such a system would present a safety hazard with the skies above us cluttered by debris.

Founder & CEO of Tesla

Elon Musk is the co-founder, CEO and product architect at Tesla Motors, a company dedicated to producing affordable, mass-market electric cars as well as battery products and solar roofs. Musk oversees all product development, engineering and design of the company's products.

Five years after its formation, in 2008, the company unveiled the Roadster, a sports car capable of accelerating from 0 to 60 mph in 3.7 seconds, as well traveling nearly 250 miles between charges of its lithium ion battery. With a stake in the company taken by Daimler and a strategic partnership with Toyota, Tesla

Motors launched its initial public offering in June 2010, raising $226 million.

Additional successes include the Model S, the company's first electric sedan. Capable of covering 265 miles between charges, the Model S was honored as the 2013 Car of the Year by Motor Trend magazine.

In April 2017, Tesla announced that it surpassed General Motors to become the most valuable U.S. car maker. The news was an obvious boon to Tesla, which was looking to ramp up production and release its Model 3 sedan later that year.

In November, Musk made another splash with the unveiling of the new Tesla Semi and Roadster at the company's design studio. The semi truck, which enters into production in 2019, boasts 500 miles of range as well as a battery and motors built to last 1 million miles. The Roadster, set to follow in 2020, will become the fastest production car ever made with its 0 to 60 time of 1.9 seconds.

After initially aiming to produce 5,000 new Model 3 cars per week by December 2017, Musk pushed that goal back to March 2018, and then to June with the start of the new year. The announced delay didn't surprise industry experts, who were well aware of the company's production problems, though some questioned how long investors would remain patient with the process. It also didn't prevent Musk from garnering a radical new compensation package as CEO, in which he would be paid after reaching milestones of growing valuation based on $50 billion increments.

By April 2018, with Tesla expected to fall short of first-quarter production forecasts, news surfaced that Musk had pushed aside the head of engineering to personally oversee efforts in that division. In a Twitter exchange with a reporter, Musk said it was important to "divide and conquer" to meet production goals and was "back to sleeping at factory."

After signaling that the company would reorganize its management structure, Musk in June announced that Tesla was laying off 9 percent of its workforce, though its production department would remain intact. In an email to employees, Musk explained his decision to eliminate some "duplication of roles" to cut costs, admitting it was time to take serious steps toward turning a profit.

The restructuring appeared to pay dividends, as it was announced that Tesla had met its goal of producing 5,000 Model 3 cars per week by the end of June, while churning out another 2,000 Model S sedans and Model X SUVs. "We did it!" Musk wrote in an celebratory email to the company. "What an incredible job by an amazing team."

SolarCity Acquisition

In August 2016, in Musk's continuing effort to promote and advance sustainable energy and products for a wider consumer base, a $2.6 billion dollar deal was solidified to combine his electric car and solar energy companies. His Tesla Motors Inc. announced an all-stock deal purchase of SolarCity Corp., a company Musk had helped his cousins start in 2006. He is a majority shareholder in each entity.

"Solar and storage are at their best when they're combined. As one company, Tesla (storage) and SolarCity (solar) can create fully integrated residential, commercial and grid-scale products that improve the way that energy is generated, stored and consumed," read a statement on Tesla's website about the deal

Mindset

How does Elon Musk think?

That's what I aimed to discover while researching the habits behind his unbelievable success. Musk is arguably the most impressive living human being on earth. For proof, here's his track record:

Oh yeah, and he's one of the few people to found multibillion dollar companies. Not bad.

The crazy part is he doesn't care that he's worth billions. In fact, he's annoyed with journalists asking about him. He wants them to ask about the bigger, worldly problems he's trying to solve. He's not focused on his existence, he's focused on the existence of humanity -- sustainable energy, clean transportation, and interplanetary space travel.

How does he think? What are his mental frameworks? What makes him tick? I scoured through dozens of interviews to unravel his six most compelling lessons ... and turned them into actionable exercises.

These lessons (and accompanying exercises) have changed my life.

Elon Musk mindset

- Seek criticism
- Challenge your existing beliefs
- Narrow your focus
- Create a back-up plan
- Practice for failure
- Have a big impact

Seek criticism

Criticism is like exercise. In the beginning, it's tough. But it slowly shapes us into healthier people and leads to many long-term benefits. While compliments create contentment, criticism creates improvement.

And when your mission for SpaceX is "interplanetary co-existence" and Tesla "transforming sustainable energy for humanity" (yes, those are Elon Musk's words), you cannot be content. For example:

"When I spoke with someone about the Tesla Model S, I didn't really want to know what's right about the car. I want to know what's wrong about the car.

When my friends get a product, I ask them to please not tell me what they like. Rather, tell me what you don't like. And if I've asked that a few times of people, then they will start automatically telling me without me having to always ask the question."

"You should take the approach that you're wrong. Your goal is to be less wrong."

Challenge reality (by understanding the fundamentals)

Einstein said, "You can't solve problems with the same thinking that caused them." Musk couldn't agree more.

For example, people have said battery packs will always be expensive, because they're expensive to make, and that's just is how it is. Yet Musk realized when you break down batteries into their fundamental components (cobalt, nickel, aluminum, carbon, polymers, and a steel can) and build your own batteries, costs go down dramatically.

This led to Tesla Energy, or revolutionary energy storage for sustainable homes and businesses. By challenging the status quo, Musk developed home energy storage that's causing radical change.

Most of us aren't creating revolutionary shifts in energy consumption. So how does this lesson apply to the rest of us? Simply put, it means questioning when someone (or yourself) says, "That's just how it is and how it's always been."

Upset the status quo. Ask tough questions. Explore the fundamental truths behind the challenges in your life. Explore how things really work by making "why" your favorite question to ask.

"Boil things down to the most fundamental truths. Then reason up from there.

- Elon Musk

Focus on signal over noise

Elon Musk isn't the only billionaire preaching the power of focus. Warren Buffet had his notorious "not-to-do list." Steve Jobs consistently preached a focused mindset by saying, "Deciding what not to do is as important as deciding what to do." And according to Noah Kagan, Facebook employee #30, Mark Zuckerberg once said, "I will not entertain ANY idea unless it helps Facebook grow the total number of users."

Musk follows the same principles. Except he will not entertain any idea beyond product development. For example, many companies put more money into marketing than they do engineering. Musk would rather minimally promote an incredible product than promote the living hell out of a mediocre one:

"At Tesla, we've never spent any money on advertising. We've put all our money into R&D, engineering, design, and manufacturing to build the best car possible. When we consider spending money, we ask, 'Will this create a better product?' If not, we don't proceed with spending the money."

Stephen Covey calls this putting first things first. Focus on what matters, ignore the rest.

"Will this activity result in a better product? If not, stop those efforts." - Elon Musk

Make failure an option (by defining a contingency plan)

I believe inaction is caused by fear. Particularly, the fear of failure. We don't apply for our dream job, because we're afraid we won't get it (which makes us feel crappy about ourselves). We don't approach the attractive person across the room, because we're afraid we'll say something stupid. We don't start a company, because we're afraid we'll waste our money and fail.

When you're starting a company with a mission for interplanetary exploration, failure is a viable option. Instead of throwing in the towel, Elon Musk anticipated failure and created a contingency plan for SpaceX:

"If we don't get the first SpaceX rocket launch to succeed by the time we've spent $100 million, we will stop the company. That will be enough for three attempted launches."

What happened to the first launch? $30 million later, it failed. The second? $60 million later, it failed. On the third and last attempt, SpaceX successfully launched. This won a $1.6 billion contract from NASA for 12 resupply flights to the station. Not bad Elon Musk, not bad at all.

Was Elon Musk afraid of failure? Absolutely. But did he create a plan to address possible failure? Yes. And that's precisely what made him put rockets into space.

"Failure is an option here. If things are not failing, you are not innovating enough." - Elon Musk

Remove worries (by living the worst-case scenario)

After defining worst-case scenarios and addressing solutions to potential problems (i.e. a contingency plan), we can still feel afraid. The best way to remove fear is by literally putting yourself in that horrible situation and asking how you feel.

For example, when Elon Musk decided he wanted to be an entrepreneur at 17 years old, he forced himself to live off $1 per day (the typical struggle of an entrepreneur). At that time, he lived mainly off hot dogs and oranges.

Elon didn't do it because he was poor. He did it to see if he had what it takes to lead the life as an entrepreneur. And since he was successful with this experiment, he knew that money wouldn't be an issue.

Experimenting with a reduced income showed Musk he could do it. This pushed him into entrepreneurship.

"I figured if I could live off a dollar a day then, at least from a food stand point, it's pretty easy to earn $30 a month." - Elon Musk

Solve Problems Beyond Yourself

Many of us (I'm guilty of this myself) focus on finding a fun, secure, and challenging job that makes us happy. We ask about the salary. About the benefits. And the culture. But are we asking if our work is making an impact on the world? Are we using today to solve tomorrow's problems? Are we forward thinking?

Elon Musk didn't ask himself, "What are some of the best ways I can make money?" Instead, as he left PayPal, he asked himself, "What are some of the problems that are likely to affect the future of humanity?"

Musk never mentions profit in interviews. He discusses SpaceX's goal to make humanity into a multi-planetary species, or Tesla's goal to accelerate the world's movement toward having most electric cars.

He solves problems not to improve his world, but the world.

"If something is important enough, even if the odds are against you, you should still do it." - Elon Musk

Business strategies

it's Elon's willingness to go big and bold that really sets him apart from most entrepreneurs. We don't need multi-million dollar budgets to learn from that. In fact, we can take some of the broader ideas and learn a lot.

Here's nine valuable lessons and good business strategies that we can learn from Elon Musk

Enter Action with Boldness

Launching the Falcon Heavy rocket into space itself was an amazing achievement. Beyond it's million dollar price tag, the Falcon Heavy is the largest rockets ever created. That, in itself, is enough to attract people to SpaceX's good business ideas. But what really made the launch unique, of course, was the car they put into space. And if that wasn't enough, they surrounded it with cameras so we could watch it on its flight... er, drive... to space. That's bold.

Consider similar good business ideas with your own Amazon business. By now, everyone knows the basics of launching an Amazon product: source it, import it, launch it, and give away some promos on JumpSend to beef up your ranking. But how can you go bold? Consider these bold and potentially good business ideas:

Effectively utilize controversy to draw attention to your product—like Cards Against Humanity.

Create some wild, non-typical images for your product listing (at least the non-main images).

When sourcing, look at what your competitors are doing and try to stand out as much as possible on the search page—if everyone's making a silver fidgetspinner, be the seller that creates the bright pink one, etc.

Make a zany video that catches buyer attention while demonstrating the product's features, like Squatty Potty did (see below).

Build Build Build

At Elon's first company after college, Zip2, he took very little from the business. He was known to sleep at his desk. He drove a cheap car. It wasn't about taking a big paycheck or "living the dream", it was about building something. .

Don't Be Afraid to Bait the Line

When PayPal, Elon's second major company, was trying to build its customer base, they offered users $5 to sign up. Who's going to say no to $5? Of course, this cost the company a ton of money, but in the end it worked out. Ebay later bought PayPal for $1.2 billion, cementing Elon Musk's position as a brilliant entrepreneur.

When launching a product on Amazon, it can be tough to cut in front of the thousands of other products and get in front of more people. The best way to do this is through instructing Amazon's search algorithm that your product is worth notice by giving away promotions. Of course, just creating a promotion isn't enough. You'll need to advertise it, too. The fastest way to do that is by putting your Amazon product onto a promotional marketing platform like Jump Send.

Have Fun With It

Elon's got a crazy sense of humor. For example, Tesla's models are S, 3, and X (get it?). He called his tunneling company The Boring Company. And let's not forget that he created a lightweight portable flamethrower and made videos of him "playing" with it. If that wasn't enough, he also put up this twitter post:

I friend of mine once said that when it comes to product research and good business ideas, it's better to sell a product that you love than one you're doing just to make crazy profits. Elon's companies have always been about changing the world. He's working on what he loves and having a ball doing it.

Create Products That Your Customers Don't Even Know They Want

- Portable flamethrowers.
- Electric cars with door handles that pop out when you get near them.
- Rockets to Mars.

Nobody asked for these things, or if they did, they could not have possibly imagined that the products would be as great as they were. These were more than just good business ideas.

Henry Ford once said, "If I gave the customers what they wanted I would have just given them faster horses." Elon Musk lives by the same philosophy.

When creating great products to sell on Amazon, of course you will want to use Jungle Scout to find great niches and profitable product opportunities. But the real key to success on Amazon is through innovation and creating what's never existed before. Whether you're bundling products that make sense as a unit, changing the color, or just having fun with something that's already there, get creative.

It's Worth It To Have a Great Team and Great Mentors

They're known as the PayPal Mafia.

Peter Thiel, Reed Hoffman, Luke Nosek, Ken Howery, Steve Chen, Chad Hurley, Jawad Karim, Max Levchin, and of course, Elon Musk.

All of these people built PayPal. And after PayPal, they all went on to do bigger and better things.

Elon Musk, of course, started Tesla and Space X.

Peter Thiel built Palantir and was one of Facebook's first equity partners.

Reid Hoffman started LinkedIn.

Max Levchin helped start Yelp.

Steve Chen, Jawad Karim, and Chad Hurley started YouTube.

Having a great team and great mentors (many of these people still assist Elon Musk today) is key to entrepreneurial success. This is something we know all too well with Jungle Scout. Many of us look up to Greg as our mentor, and even Greg has mentors of his own that he follows.

Being an Entrepeneur is Hard Work, But Worth It

There's a great quote from Elon Musk that occasionally makes its rounds on social media.

Now, that isn't meant to scare people off.

In fact, when Elon originally said it at the Founder's Forum. he followed up with a "evil" laugh. And it's true, being an entrepreneur is hard work. Yet, having a good sense of humor about the trials and tribulations you'll face an entrepreneur–especially if you're an Amazon seller, is simply a good business idea.

8 – Begin With the End in Mind

Elon Musk wants to retire on Mars.

Which is a pretty bold goal considering we've yet to even put a man or woman on Mars, let alone have the resources to allow someone to retire on it.

But Elon is fully aware of this. Therefore, everything he does with SpaceX, Tesla, and all his other companies works towards that goal of retiring on a lifeless lump of red rock 54.6 million kilometers away.

Sometimes it can seem like things are as far away as Mars. But it's the little steps that matter.

In one of my favorite books, Gary Keller and Jay Papasan's The One Thing, Keller and Papasan encourage that we chase the big goals. Once we know where we're going–whether it's a 7-figure Amazon business or a retirement cottage at the edge of Valles Marineris–we can start working our way back from that goal.

THE ONE THING'S GOAL SETTING STRATEGY. IT COULD PUT YOU ON MARS!

Working backwards from a "someday" goal.

The process is simple. First, state your goal. Then, break it down into smaller bites.

"Some day I want to be a 7-figure Amazon seller."

Okay, so what do you need to do in the next five years to reach that point?

"I need to have 100 SKUs each earning an average of $833 in net profit each month."

Okay, so what do you need to do in the next year to reach that point?

"I need to have researched and sourced at least 1 profitable product that can earn an average of $833/month in net profits."

Okay, so what do you need do in the next week to reach that point?

"I need to track at least 100 unique products to sell on Amazon."

Okay, so what do you need to do today to reach that point?

"I need to research at least 15 products."

Okay, so what do you need to do RIGHT NOW?

"I need to start working

It's really that simple.

Learn As Much As You Can

Did you know that Elon Musk taught himself rocket science.

Literally. He taught himself ROCKET SCIENCE. And he did it through reading textbooks and speaking to industry heavyweights.

One of SpaceX's engineers Jim Cantrell, a rocket scientist himself, was blown away by Elon's determination to learn as much as he can about what he was doing. "He knows everything about what he's building," said Cantrell. "He is the smartest guy I've ever met, period," Cantrell said. "I know that sounds overblown. But I've met plenty of smart people, and I don't say that lightly. He's absolutely, frickin' amazing. I don't even think he sleeps."

Now, that's not to say that we've all got to go out and memorize textbooks on rocket propulsion and astrodynamics. But it definitely pays to have a good mind for all the different elements that goes into operating a business. Those are good business ideas whether you're building rockets for the government or selling fidget-spinners on Amazon.

Richard Branson (Virgin, Aeroplanes, space travel, music)

Sir Richard Branson biography, an English entrepreneur, investor and the founder of Virgin Group, which includes more than 400 companies in 30 countries from the entirely different industries.

Nobody knows the exact number of businesses managed by Virgin Group. Some say that even Richard Branson is not able to answer how many business ideas are implemented under the wing of his multi-brand. However, the charm of its business is not in the quantities of the companies but in the quality of services provided.

Richard Branson is an extraordinary personality, mainly known to the general public for his non-standard actions, including the creation of his reality show, The Rebel Billionaire: Branson's Quest for the Best, and numerous attempts to break world speed records, including the fastest ever Atlantic Ocean crossing. A hippie-billionaire, a master of shocking, a nail in the boot of big business, an iron fist in a velvet glove, Richard "The Robber" Branson, knighted by the Prince of Wales with the Knight Bachelor title for his "services to entrepreneurship" – it is all about Sir Richard Branson.

The distinctive personality traits of Richard Branson are self-confidence, high level of humility, trustworthiness, authenticity, enthusiasm, optimism, and warmth.

Personal history

Richard Charles Nicholas Branson was born on July 18, 1950, in Surrey, England. The family did not have a steady income at the time as his father Edward had failed his bar exams and did not have a qualification to work. The three could often be seen riding a motorcycle with Richard in the sidecar and Eve riding pillion, reciting legal cases into Edward's ear.

Richard's sister Lindi was born in 1953. By this time, Richard's father had finally qualified as a barista while Eve assisted with the income from her self-made embroidered cushions and trinkets she sold at Harrods.

An enormous merit in Richard's formation as a person belongs to his mother, Eve Branson. Evette felt that something was going wrong since Richard's birth: from the early years his motor coordination was strongly impaired, and it was often impossible actually to understand what he was saying – sometimes the letters and numbers were meaningless for him. Later, doctors diagnosed Richard Branson with myopia and dyslexia. Usually, people who suffer from dyslexia cannot learn to read and write during all their life, but Evette did not give up and prudently cared about Richard's adoption to the real life.

Eve periodically arranged challenges for Richard: he had to go I know not whither and fetch I know not what. Usually, he succeeded. When Branson was only four years old, she dropped him off the car a few miles away from home and told him to look for his dad across the fields. A little boy found him in the same evening.

When Richard was eleven, she woke him up an early January morning, gave him a bicycle, put an apple and a few sandwiches in a bag and sent him to relatives who lived in a town fifty miles away from Richard's home. Richard had to get some water by himself along the way. He came back proud and tired; he was very pleased about that and Eve immediately sent him on an errand.

They never had a TV set nor listened to the radio, but Branson recalled his childhood fun and happy. His parents loved each other and treated Ricky and his two sisters as equals. Eve Branson was sure that one day her son would become prime minister, and was doing everything for that he would not blunder when it is time to ascend to the top. She had no doubt that her son was up for everything.

In his early childhood, Richard Branson met Nik Powell, who became his best friend for life. Their friendship was inseparable, and it had elements of competition as they enjoyed making challenges for each other. When they were eight, they were separated. Richard was sent to Scaitcliffe School, a boarding preparatory school in Berkshire. Later, Nik Powell would become one of the early pioneers of Virgin Group. For Richard Branson, who suffered from dyslexia, education turned into torture. He was unable to read, write or spell well and was often beaten for poor behavior.

Richard's father went to boarding school and his father before him, so it was a traditional practice for the family. Richard hated it because he always got into trouble and struggled in class. Aged 8, he still could not read and could not make out the letters and numbers on the blackboard. Richard had dyslexia.

Back then, no one knew or cared about it which meant that the rest of the class and the teachers just thought he was lazy.

To contrast his poor academic performance, Richard proved to be remarkably good at sports. He notes that if you were good at sports at an English school, you were the hero, and the schoolmasters didn't care if you failed all of your exams. Richard became the captain of the football, rugby, and cricket teams. He won every race and unintentionally set a new record for the long jump after deciding just to give it a try. The fun lasted until the first injury that Richard received playing football. The doctor told him that he could not play sports for a very long time, and he was back in the classroom hitting rock bottom and being the worst on every subject.

Richard went to another school on the Sussex coast called Cliff View House where he was to prepare for the Common Entrance exam. This school had no sports. It was the place where you would get beat for not remembering a math formula. Dyslexia was no longer an excuse, as they got beat for nearly anything. Dirty shoes? Beat. Are you walking a little faster than you should be? Beat. Not making your beds properly? Talking when you should be ⬜uiet? Beat, beat, beat.

Perhaps the only pleasant memory from that school was the headmaster's lovely daughter Charlotte. She liked Richard, and the two had a routine of nightly visits until Richard got busted by one of his teachers. The headmaster summoned him to his study and asked what he was doing at his house. Richard replied with: "I was on my way back from your daughter's room, sir." The headmaster then expelled him from school.

That very evening, to escape the anger of his parents, Richard wrote a pretend suicide note. He put it in an envelope and gave it to a boy, instructing him not to open it until the next day, knowing that he definitely would. As he slowly made his way through the school grounds towards the cliffs, he saw a crowd of teachers and students running after him. They dragged him back from the cliff and annulled the expulsion. Richard's parents were surprisingly calm about the case.

After Cliff View House beat Richard into shape, he moved to Stowe School in 1963. It was a big public school in Buckinghamshire with over 800 boys. Richard's struggle with the academic system continued at Stowe School. His knee injury would not allow him to sprint and participate in sports, and he was just a bad in class as he was at the previous schools. The library was his sanctuary, where he spent his afternoons writing a novel about a hopeless schoolboy expertly seduced by a young and lascivious school matron.

The other frequenter at the library was the sophisticated and widely read Jonathan Holland-Gems. Jonathan helped Richard develop a passion for journalism and newspapers. Richard thought that he even might like to become a journalist. Soon, he took part in a school essay competition and won.

Business background

Richard Charles Nicholas Branson was born on July 18, 1950, in Surrey, England. His father, Edward James Branson, worked as a barrister. His mother, Eve Branson, was employed as a flight attendant. Richard, who struggled with dyslexia, had a hard time with educational institutions. He nearly failed out of the all-boys Scaitcliffe School, which he attended until the age of 13. He then transferred to Stowe School, a boarding school in Stowe, Buckinghamshire, England.

Still struggling, Branson dropped out at the age of 16 to start a youth-culture magazine called Student. The publication, run by students, sold $8,000 worth of advertising in its first edition, launched in 1966. The first run of 50,000 copies was disseminated for free, with Branson afterward covering the costs through advertising.

By 1969, Branson was living in a London commune, surrounded by the British music and drug scene. It was during this time that Branson had the idea to begin a mail-order record company called Virgin to help fund his magazine efforts. The company performed modestly but well enough for Branson to expand his business venture, with a record shop on Oxford Street, London. With the success of the new store, the high school dropout was able to build a recording studio in 1972 in Oxfordshire, England.

Virgin Records

The first artist on the Virgin Records label, Mike Oldfield, recorded his single "Tubular Bells" in 1973 with the help of Branson's team. The song was an instant smash, staying on the

UK charts for 247 weeks. Using the momentum of Oldfield's success, Branson then signed other aspiring musical groups to the label, including the Sex Pistols. Artists such as the Culture Club, the Rolling Stones and Genesis would follow, helping to make Virgin Music one of the top six record companies in the world.

Business Expansion

Branson expanded his entrepreneurial efforts yet again, this time to include the Voyager Group travel company in 1980, the Virgin Atlantic airline in 1984 and a series of Virgin Megastores. However, Branson's success was not always predictable, and by 1992, Virgin was suddenly struggling to stay financially afloat. The company was sold later that year to Thorn EMI for $1 billion.

Branson was crushed by the loss, reportedly crying after the contract was signed, but remained determined to stay in the music business. In 1993, he founded the station Virgin Radio, and in 1996 he started a second record company, V2, which signed artists such as Powder Finger and Tom Jones.

The Virgin Group eventually reached 35 countries around the world, with nearly 70,000 employees handling affairs in the United Kingdom, the United States, Australia, Canada, Asia, Europe, South Africa and beyond. He has expanded his businesses to include a train company, a luxury game preserve, a mobile phone company and a space-tourism company, Virgin Galactic.

Branson is also known for his sporting achievements, notably the record-breaking Atlantic crossing in Virgin Atlantic Challenger II in 1986, and the first crossing by hot-air balloon of the Atlantic (1987) and Pacific (1991). He was knighted in 1999 for his contribution to entrepreneurship, and in 2009, he landed at No. 261 on Forbes' "World Billionaires" list with his $2.5 billion in self-made fortune, including two private islands.

Virgin Galactic, Voyages and Hotels

In recent years, the ever-adventurous Branson has focused much of his attention on his space-tourism venture. He partnered with Scaled Composites to form The Spaceship Company, which set to work developing a suborbital spaceplane. In April 2013, the project made an impressive leap forward with the test launch of SpaceShipTwo.

Branson was delighted by the success of his spaceship's first test, telling NBC News that "We're absolutely delighted that it broke the sound barrier on its very first flight, and that everything went so smoothly." By April 2013, more than 500 people had reserved tickets to ride on a Virgin Galactic spaceship.

In 2015, Branson announced the launch of Virgin Voyages, a new cruise line. On October 31, 2017, the company commemorated the milestone of laying down the keel for its first ship. Virgin's cruise ships, designed to hold 2,800 guests and a crew of 1,150, remained on track to debut in 2020.

Additionally, the mogul moved forward with his upstart Virgin Hotels, founded in 2010. In 2018, Virgin announced its presence in Las Vegas by taking over ownership of the Hard Rock Hotel. The company planned to generally maintain the status quo in the hotel before embarking on renovations in 2019.

Mindset

Richard Branson, the billionaire CEO of Virgin Group, has it made. He has a net worth of roughly $5 billion and presides over more than 400 companies operating under the Virgin umbrella. Branson has also been knighted at Buckingham Palace and has plans to start sending paying customers to space. Needless to say, he's a wildly interesting (and incredibly rich) guy.

Like other members of the billionaire club, his success has earned him a following. People are always keeping tabs on what Bill Gates or Warren Buffett are up to, in an effort to mirror them and capitalize for themselves. But like them, Richard Branson is seemingly from a different planet than most of us. It's hard to say just what exactly the "X-factor" is, but if it were as simple as copying what other people did, we'd all have piles of money.

Fortunately, guys like Buffett and Branson are willing to share some insights into their thinking and processes. Buffett may tell us his tricks to investing, or which books to read, for example. Branson, on the other hand, is willing to talk more about his mindset. That is, the method of thinking that helped him achieve such wild success.

In a recent blog post on the Virgin site, Branson laid it all out: "We all need growth mindsets," he wrote.

What the hell is a "growth mindset", and how do you get one? As Branson explains, it's a fairly simple concept. "This means being willing to learn, being happy to make mistakes, being eager to experiment," he wrote.

"Far too many young people are taught to think with fixed mindsets: concentrating on exams, worrying about failing, wonderfully multi-shaped talents fretting about fitting into square holes," Branson said. He then brought up the definition of growth mindset as put forth by his family's organization, Big Change.

Quoting Big Change, Branson wrote the following:

A growth mindset isn't simply a positive mindset. This isn't just about being happy. It is about a fundamental belief that you can grow, learn and change for the better – through failure and success alike. This mindset motivates you to try, to reflect, to get back up, to ask for help and to learn. Ultimately changed minds is what brings about a big change.

So, there you have it. Branson attributes much of his success to his ability to adopt this way of thinking. It's an ability to evolve and adapt as you go. To take on tasks that may end in failure, but not fearing that failure — everything is a lesson. Using those lessons, you can approach challenges from a different angle.

Think like a billionaire

Branson's growth mindset has propelled him to the upper echelons of society. And you can see how others have used that growth mindset to achieve great things as well — even if they don't identify it specifically. We can look at some of the world's most powerful and businesses as examples.

Take Mark Zuckerberg. Facebook has grown from a mere social media network to so much more. These days, it's a (reluctant, perhaps) news platform. It's a marketplace. The company has grown well beyond anything its founders probably envisioned. The reason it continues to do so is because the company's leadership has abandoned a rigid mindset. It tries new things and learns from failures.

You can say the same about Apple, or Google. All of these companies were founded and run by people who are now billionaires. Think about the billionaires or super successful people out there. A list that includes the aforementioned Buffett, Gates, and Zuckerberg. But also Jeff Bezos, Phil Knight, and Paul Allen. All of them had to have a growth mindset to make it.

Do you think everything Nike's put out has been a hit? Or that Amazon became a massive worldwide company by following a straight trajectory?

By adopting a different way of thinking, like the one that Branson lays out, we can become more agile. We can treat mistakes as lessons. And if we play our cards right, shorten our trip to the top substantially

Business strategies

He's generous, too. In a recent blog post, Branson gives readers a peek into how he got where is he today by sharing his top 10 secrets to success. Anyone can learn from his advice, whether you're founding your third company or starting out as as intern.

1. Follow your dreams

You'll never be successful if you don't love what you do and wake up every morning excited. "Those people who spend their time working on things they love are usually the ones enjoying life the most," Branson says. "They are also the ones who dared to take a risk and chase their dreams."

Legendary investor and fellow billionaire Warren Buffett agrees. "Being successful at almost anything means having a passion for it," he said during a recent conversation with Bill Gates. "If you see somebody with even reasonable intelligence and a terrific passion for what they do and who can get people around them to march, even when those people can't see over the top of the next hill, things are gonna happen."

2. Do some good

According to Branson, "if you aren't making a positive difference to other people's lives, then you shouldn't be in business." This goes not only for individuals, but companies as a whole, Branson says.

Today, many employers ascribe to this idea. Take companies like Toms and Warby Parker, which follow the "One for One" or

"Buy a Pair, Give a Pair" rule: Every time a pair of shoes or glasses is purchased, one is donated.

3. Believe in your ideas

If you aren't advocating for yourself, you're not giving anyone else a reason to. As Branson says, "If you aren't proud of your idea and believe in your plans, why should anybody else?"

Fellow billionaire Mark Cuban has similar views on what it takes to succeed, particularly for entrepreneurs. "Don't start a company unless it's an obsession and something you love," he wrote in a column on Entrepreneur. Because, "if you have an exit strategy, it's not an obsession."

4. Have fun

Though often underrated, Branson calls fun one of the most important ingredients in any successful business. "If you're not having fun, then it's probably time to try something else," he writes.

The concept of having fun has driven some of Branson's most successful businesses, especially when he was first starting out. When he went to the CEOs of Virgin Music with the idea of using a third of the company's profits to start an airline because he believed it would be "fun," they weren't entirely on board, Business Insider reports. But Branson persisted and Virgin Atlantic, one of the company's most well-known properties, was born.

5. Don't give up

"On every adventure I have been on — whether setting up a business, flying around the world in a balloon or racing across the ocean in a boat — there have been moments when the easy thing to do would be to give up," Branson writes. But, by sticking things through, he's propelled himself to immense success, both personal and professional.

Branson's onto something with this tip. Psychologist and MacArthur "Genius" fellow Angela Duckworth spent years researching achievement, and found that talent by itself is only one factor. Success also requires determined effort, and lots of it.

"Without effort, your talent is nothing more than your unmet potential," Duckworth writes in her book, "Grit: The Power of Passion and Perseverance."

6. Keep setting new challenges

"If you don't write down your ideas, they could be gone by the morning," Branson says. He solves this problem himself by making lists of every kind, from ideas for companies to upcoming plans.

"Write down every single idea you have, no matter how big or small," he wrote in a blog post. And then challenge yourself to follow through. You never know what's going to hit.

7. Learn to delegate

Learning that you don't have to do everything yourself is a difficult skill for many entrepreneurs, but it's worth it. "If you find people who can take on tasks you aren't good at, it frees you up to plan for the future," Branson writes.

Refusing to delegate also limits your financial potential, says Keith Cameron Smith in "The Top 10 Distinctions Between Millionaires and the Middle Class." "Having a belief that no one can do it as well as you is ignorance. The world is full of talented people," he writes.

Stop stressing that something won't be done correctly if you don't have a hand in it and start putting more faith into the people who work for and under you. Delegate! That might even improve the outcome. As Smith writes, "[Millionaires] believe they can find someone who can do it not only as well as they can, but even better!"

8. Look after your team

Your personal success matters, but so does the success of your team. Branson points out the importance of fostering a welcoming, safe and innovative work environment: "If your staff are having fun and genuinely care about other people, they will enjoy their work more and do a better job."

It's also crucial to hire the right people. "Find people who look for the best in others, praise rather than criticise, and love what they do," Branson writes.

9. Get out there

Success — and adventure — isn't going to come to you. You've got to go find it. "Rather than sitting in front of a screen all your life, switch off the TV or the computer and go out into the world," Branson says.

Taking a break from work also gives you a chance to relax and recharge. Going on regular vacations can mitigate burnout and even help boost your chances of getting a raise.

10. When people say bad things about you, prove them wrong

To thrive, you must be prepared for critics and copycats.

"Some people will react to success by trying to hang onto your coat tails," Branson warns. "The best thing you can do is to not only ignore them, but to prove them wrong in every single way."

Conclusion

We know that billionaires are a unique type of people. All billionaires in the world share these specific mindsets about wealth that ordinary people don't. While adopting these mindsets doesn't imply you'll become a billionaire in your lifetime, it will certainly create for you a foundation in your own mind from where you can begin accumulating wealth and that can make all the difference. Ultimately, it is up to you to change your circumstances.

In conclusion, billionaires are careful spenders, tough investors and love taking risks. Study their habits, learn from them and develop the same habits. And remember, getting rich is easy. However, staying rich requires hard work. On top of that, when you suddenly become rich it can suddenly disappear. Don't strive to become a billionaire if you haven't got the right mindset to live like one.

Disclaimer

The information contained within this eBook is strictly for educational purposes. If you wish to apply ideas contained in this eBook, you are taking full responsibility for your actions.

The author has made every effort to ensure the accuracy of the information within this book was correct at time of publication. The author does not assume and hereby disclaims any liability to any party for any loss, damage, or disruption caused by errors or omissions, whether such errors or omissions result from accident, negligence, or any other cause.

(sucess, self help)

About The Author

My name is MARY DAVENPORT, I am the founder and owner of THE ACT OF CREATIVITY (TAOC).

I am first and foremost a mother of 3, grandmother of 8. Have been freelancing for many years now , as a writer before I setup my own organization, i am also currently an hotel general manager and an avid reader..my favorite is kindle publishing though..lol I really love educating people on how to become successful in life, stay healthy and live the life of their dreams

Do not go yet; One last thing to do

If you enjoyed this book or found it useful I'd be very grateful if you'd post a short review on it. Your support really does make a difference and I read all the reviews personally so I can get your feedback and make this book even better.

Thanks again for your support!

www.ingramcontent.com/pod-product-compliance
Lightning Source LLC
Chambersburg PA
CBHW031543210526
45464CB00003B/1121